Courageous - Honest - Loyal - Compassionate - Kind

Believe-in
Your Inner Warrior

Bravery - Strength - True to You - Belief – Empathy – Giving - Helpful

Written & Illustrated
by S. V. Davies

HEDDON PUBLISHING

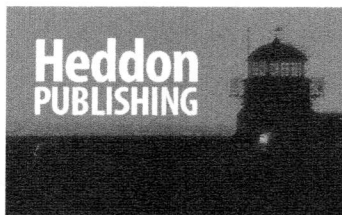

www.heddonpublishing.com

www.facebook.com/heddonpublishing

@PublishHeddon

Dedicated to my children,

who I believe have inner warriors inside them

so that they can overcome any difficulty, any pain,

and conquer any war!

Love you to the moon and back! MB

To Sonny
Believe-in yourself &
all that you are!
love
S

About Sue Davies

First and foremost, I am a mother of three. I am also a nana.

I trained in children's yoga in 2014 and went on to study and progress with family and community yoga, adult hatha yoga teaching, transformational hatha yoga, restorative yoga, parent and baby yoga, mindfulness teacher training & healing trauma through yoga.

I am passionate about the benefits of yoga and know how the techniques which I have learned can also help children and young people.

Through the **Believe-in** stories I hope to teach children and young people the tools and techniques they can use to cope with challenging situations: to **Believe-in** themselves and the resources they have inside of them!

My hope is that my books will be enjoyed by parents along with their children.

I hope you like them

x Sue

www.believe-in.co.uk

Welcome to

Believe-in

Your Inner Warrior

At some point in their lives, everybody will experience hurt or pain inflicted on them by another person – whether intentionally or unintentionally.

You can imagine each time you are hurt as if you are being hit by an arrow.

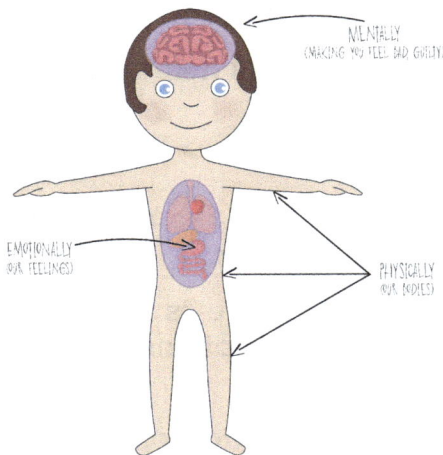

There are many places and ways each arrow can hit, producing different types of injury:

- Mentally (being made to feel guilty, or sad)

- Physically (causing physical pain to our bodies)

- Emotionally (damaging our feelings)

Each injury can make us feel scared, fearful, ashamed, anxious, and very alone.

It is easy to feel that you are the only person in your situation but many other people are experiencing hurtful things at the same time, in different ways.

The people firing the arrows do so for many different reasons. It is important to understand that this is NOT your fault.

We may not be able to stop people firing arrows but what we can do is learn how to respond to and deal with them, protecting and healing ourselves.

The 1st step is to acknowledge to ourselves that this person has hurt us with the arrows they fired.

The 2nd step is that we need to recognise the hurt caused and our feelings, and show kindness towards ourselves to help begin the healing process.

Within ourselves, we have the power to prevent the person causing more pain and hurt to ourselves, and other people. But this takes courage, and bravery.

I believe that all of this is inside all of us! Yes – that includes YOU!!

Through our **Believe-in** stories, following the exercises and activities, you can learn about yourself and find important tools that can help you discover the warrior inside you.

In **Believe-in** Your Inner Warrior, we meet Jamie.

Jamie is being hurt by arrows which cause physical, emotional and mental pain.

We are going to work with Jamie, to find ways to deal with this, and to find the inner warrior who will help to gather allies, form an army, and stop the hurt continuing.

Then together we will learn how to begin to heal.

But first, it's important to realise that even warriors have rules….

While you are learning and practising yoga, these rules will help to keep you and your body safe:

Use your body, your mind and your breath. It sounds like a lot to think about but with a bit of practice you'll soon get used to it.

Follow the instructions as closely as possible. There is no 'perfect' movement, just safe or unsafe movements. The instructions will help to make sure you are acting in a safe way.

STOP if you feel any pain or discomfort. Listening to, respecting, and looking after your body puts you in control. Always try not to do anything that can hurt yourself physically, emotionally or mentally.

Be yourself. You may be reading this book with another person. It is important to remember that we are all different. Your body is yours, and unique to you! Try not to copy or push your body to be like anyone else. Yoga is about living in your body and accepting and loving what your body can do. This shows yourself TRUE respect as your body is individual and amazing as it is!

Use this book in the right way for you. If you need lots of practice with one of the exercises, or don't feel comfortable with another, that is absolutely fine. It is your book, and your body.

Practise! The more you practice the activities and exercises in this book, the stronger your inner warrior will become. You will learn to understand yourself more and know what is right for you! With that comes empowerment; you can win any battle.

HAVE FUN and ENJOY YOURSELF! This story is all for You!

Take care

Sue x

Believe-in
Your Inner Warrior

Believe-in your... inner warrior

Hello! I'm Jamie. I am eleven years old.

I live with my: AMAZING! mum
                Two brothers
                A dog called Violet
                A jumping fish

                Yes, a jumping fish. Honestly!

                Here's a little bit about me:

Things I **LOVE**
Drawing
Playing sports (I'm really fast!)
Hanging out with my mates

Things I **HATE, HATE, HATE!**
Homework
Mushrooms (urgh)
Early mornings

I also definitely **HATE** ☹ a certain someone (not naming names) who, well, **hurts** me. Even though I haven't done anything to them, they make my life **miserable** and **horrible** when they're around.

I don't mind school, in fact I have a few really good friends now. My best friends are Robin, Sammy and Alex ☺.

My life seems to be a mixture of good and bad days.

The **good days** are the ones I spend with my mates, just hanging out together, messing around. We laugh a lot and it makes me feel **great**.

There are **horrible** days, too. I don't like to think of them but I know I'm becoming **snappy** at my mum. It's all because of that person I mentioned before, the one who hurts me. I can't see a way to stop them.

They said that if I tell anyone, they will just make my life worse and that nobody will believe me anyway. All I can do is try to avoid them but sometimes they get in my way, on purpose. It makes my stomach **hurt** to think about it.

I am starting to get **suspicious** of people unless I know them really well.

But I am trying to put the bad stuff out of my mind. I try and think about the **good days** instead.

At school, we have started to have lessons from a yoga teacher. Last week was all about feelings.

Apparently, our bodies pick up on lots of different things all around us. The teacher says our bodies speak to us, which sounds a bit weird. She says that it can help us if we 'tune into' ourselves daily to see what our bodies are trying to tell us… she's been showing us how we can do this.

We either sit or lie down and listen. We have to think about different parts of our bodies in turn, starting with the toes and working our way up.

If we feel anything we don't like… **sadness**, **anger**, **fear**, or just general **yuckiness**, we can help those feelings go away (or 'release' them). To do this we need to acknowledge them with **kindness** and **compassion** by saying, for example: "I understand that I am feeling **empty** and **sad** in my belly, I release these feelings with **kindness**."

I was so relieved that she didn't make us say these things out loud, it feels strange enough saying them in your head.

Then the teacher started talking about breathing – as if it's not something we've been doing all our lives!
I'm a bit of an expert at it, actually. In… out… in… out…

Once the teacher explained, though, I could see how this type of breathing was different. It's not like we usually think about our breathing much but the teacher said that if we do, it can make us feel better. Different breathing does different things to your body.

The first thing we had to do was really simple.
First of all, we had to find somewhere comfortable to sit.
I liked sitting cross-legged on the floor, but Sammy and some of the others wanted to sit on chairs. Robin decided to lie down – typical, always wanting to do things differently! The teacher said it was fine, as long as we were all comfortable.

We got handouts of all the new things we tried so I'm going to share them with you.

BREATHING ACTIVITY 1

Find somewhere comfortable to sit.

Think about your breathing.

Where can you feel your breath inside your body? In your:
Nose?
Mouth?
Throat?
Upper chest?
Lower chest?
Belly?

Can you tell if your breath is warm or cool air?
Don't worry if you can't; just notice any feelings you do have right now.

Once you are happy doing this, you could try closing your eyes, to help you look inward to your feelings.

You are already starting to get to know yourself better.

After we had all had a few goes at the first exercise, the teacher said we were doing really well and could try something a little more interesting.

We could stay in the same positions or find something different. We all stayed where we were but Robin decided it would be funny to lie down, legs in the air against the wall.

The teacher smiled and said that Robin in fact was now demonstrating a restorative relaxing yoga pose! Robin looked at us and smiled! Hahaha, trust Robin!

BREATHING EXERCISE 2: Full Belly Breathing

Imagine a balloon where your belly is. (Choose any colour you like for your balloon.)

As you inhale, let your breath inflate the balloon, filling it up.
As you exhale, slowly let all the air out of your balloon, as it deflates.

You can try repeating this three or four times before returning to your normal breathing rhythm.

Now you might want to try to tune back in with your body.
Do you notice any differences or new feelings?

The more you tune in, the better you can read your body, and feelings and thoughts.

The teacher said that sometimes people can feel as though their mind is jumping from one thing to another, like a naughty monkey jumping from one tree to another! This is perfectly normal and with practice you can learn to help **calm** your mind and focus more easily.

We were given another breathing exercise to try. For this one we needed to be sitting up. It was called **Left-Nostril Breathing**. It sounded weird and we all laughed. The teacher said that it was a great way to slow your thoughts down, and that it's also a fantastic help if you're **frightened**, **nervous** or **upset**.

This got my interest as I am **frightened** sometimes, when 'you know who' is around or I know that I am going to see them. I started to wonder if yoga might be a good way to deal with some of the feelings I have.

BREATHING EXERCISE 3: Left-Nostril Breathing

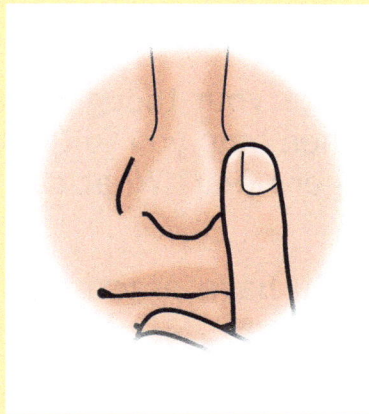

Use your first finger and place against your right nostril, closing it off.
Inhale, through your left nostril, and exhale slowly – you can do this up to ten times.

Remove the finger which is pressing on your right nostril, then close your eyes – you can try and tune into your feelings to see if you notice any difference.

The teacher told us that when a person feels **scared**, **nervous** or very **worried**, their mind can send a signal to their body that it is in **DANGER**.

This can cause it to go into '**fight**, *flight* or **FREEZE**' mode, which is perfectly normal.

It can feel uncomfortable as your heart will race and you might become short of breath and sweaty. This can be very scary! However, it is not going to **hurt** you. The teacher said that it is your body's way of trying to protect you.

What I thought was quite strange was that apparently your mind can get confused sometimes and send the same signal to your body, which causes the same reaction when there is no danger... this is sometimes known as an **anxiety** or **panic attack**.

I think I know what that feels like. I can start to feel really **anxious** about 'you know who' even if they are not around. I feel sweaty, and it feels like my heart is beating too fast, and like I'm not breathing properly.

The handout from the teacher says that our bodies hold memory too and feelings can be stored in the body. For example, stress can be stored in necks and shoulders, making them feel tight.

I listened carefully, but I didn't want my friends to realise as they don't really know anything is wrong. I could see Robin was fidgeting, and probably desperate to make a joke or something. I smiled at Robin quickly but I really didn't want to miss what the teacher was saying.

Luckily, with the handout of the exercises we practised, we got some notes, including how to deal with a panic attack.

How to deal with a panic attack

A great way to help you take control is using the deep-breathing technique you have just practised. This will send a message back to the brain to help it become calm.

You can also try to ask yourself a question that moves your thoughts to a different part of your brain to answer. That will then help you to think more clearly. Try asking yourself: WHAT is the danger I fear? What can I do to calm myself?

You could also try using left-nostril breathing if you have practised it and feel comfortable with it.

Performing breathing exercises is the best way to calm your central nervous system, and will help you think more clearly and calm you should you need to.

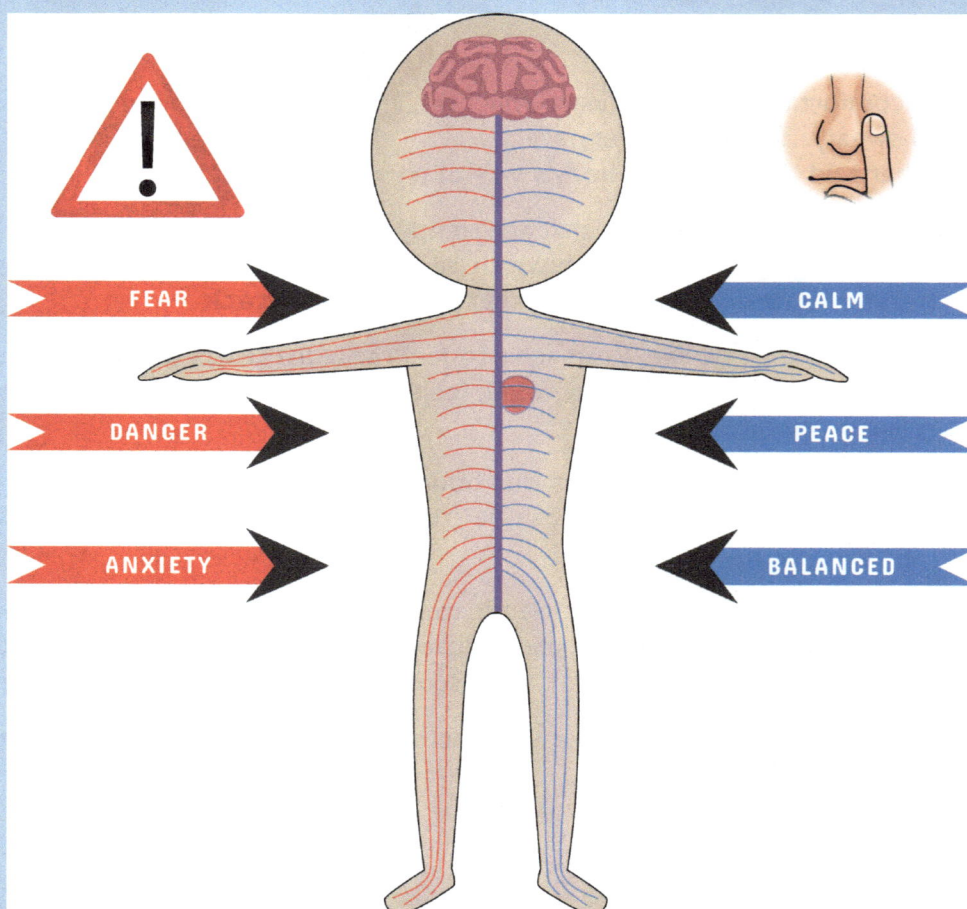

We also got some yoga homework, as if we don't have enough work to do already!

But I actually didn't mind this homework; it was to practise tuning into our bodies before and after the breathing exercises, then make a note of our findings in a diary. We had to write down how we felt before and after doing the exercises.

The teacher said that diaries can be a great way of letting feelings out; things you don't feel **happy** or **safe** saying to other people. You can name, or label, your feelings and learn more about how you feel at different times. It was hard not to judge my feelings and just let them be, as some were **upsetting**. I tried labelling them with **kindness** and **understanding**. This seemed to help.

When I have good days, I have noticed that I like my body and how I feel – so alive!

I was worried that labelling my bad feelings might make me feel worse. I usually just try to block them out, as if they're not happening. The feeling I get of a knot in my stomach: tight, **sicky** and humpy inside. But I didn't feel any worse, which was a relief!

The handout from the teacher said that we store emotions in different parts of the body, just like the brain stores information in different places. It might seem easier to turn away from negative feelings and emotions, and pretend that they are not there, but that won't make them go away.

By tuning in to our bodies, recognising our feelings, and labelling them with **kindness** when we find them, we are actually taking over some of the control that these negative emotions can have over us.

The teacher explained about us also having feelings called 'gut feelings', which we can feel in our bellies. These can help tell us if something is wrong!

Our bodies are amazing. They can pick up on all sorts of different things around us, including energies, and can sometimes register a feeling before our brain has had time to process it.

I have learned a lot about my breathing (how I can feel it more in my throat?), my feelings, and now gut feelings too!

BREATHING DIARY

Day	How I feel before breathing exercise	How I feel after breathing exercise
MONDAY	I feel a bit sick	I feel like I'm floating
TUESDAY	I feel OK	I feel a bit better, kind of empty
WEDNESDAY	I'm not really sure. I am **scared**, maybe **angry**	**Calm**, not thinking about the bad stuff
THURSDAY	Buzzing, I've just been swimming	Tired, and heavy. **Relaxed.**
FRIDAY:	**Happy**, **excited**, been talking about my birthday!	**Peaceful**, clear-headed
SATURDAY	**Anxious**, **upset**, it's been a bad day today	A bit **calmer**, and not as worried
SUNDAY	Achy back, I did a big bike ride.	Aches all gone! I feel **good**.

Here's a breathing diary you can use if you'd like to have a go:

Day	How I feel before breathing exercise	How I feel after breathing exercise
MONDAY		
TUESDAY		
WEDNESDAY		
THURSDAY		
FRIDAY:		
SATURDAY		
SUNDAY		

This week in yoga class we've been focusing on the physical exercises. The teacher says that these can help us cultivate our inner warriors, learn how to protect ourselves ➶ from arrows of pain, and to fight against problems. I liked the sound of that.

There are some weird names to the movements in yoga like Cat, Cow and Dog. Robin was laughing about them. I wanted to laugh too, but I also really wanted to listen.

We were reminded of the rules of yoga at the start of every exercise session:

- Use your body, your mind and your breath.
- Follow the instructions as closely as possible.
- STOP if you feel any pain or discomfort.
- Be yourself.
- Use this book in the right way for you.
- Practise!
- HAVE FUN and ENJOY YOURSELF!

I loved this week's lesson. I love the idea of being a warrior. The lesson started with something called Child's Pose. We were told that when faced with a war or battle, sometimes our first response is to hide, protecting ourselves, blocking out the pain....

PHYSICAL ACTIVITY 1: Child's Pose

If you would like to, you can start by kneeling on the floor or a comfy yoga mat. When you're comfy, you can rest your bottom back onto the heels of your feet.

Try curling forward, maybe rest your head on your hands or on the floor or mat your choice - whichever is comfortable for you.

You can also choose where you would like to place your hands: by the sides of your body or outstretched in front of you. You can always try both and see how your body feels.
When you find a position you like, you can rest and count for up to four breaths. When you are ready, slowly roll up your spine and come back to sitting.

The next positions had animal names, which made me want to laugh! We had to be cats and cows. The teacher said doing these movements were like having a slinky for a spine and would keep our spines healthy so I listened more...

PHYSICAL ACTIVITY 2: Cow/Cat/Cow

The starting position is called the **Cow**. If you want to start to do this movement, come onto all fours, with your tail end (bottom) up, your belly downward and head up. Maybe take a breath here and tune in to how this feels for you.

When you are ready, you can roll up your spine from your tail end (bottom) and, moving along up the spine, try arching your back to the shoulders, maybe dropping your head down. See how that feels, as you become like a **Cat** being stroked.
If you like, take a breath. You can see if this feels different to being in the **Cow** position.

When you want to, you can try returning to the **Cow** position by lifting your head slowly and rolling your slinky spine slowly back so that your belly is downward, towards the floor, and your tail end raised once more.

How did that feel for you?
If you like those movements, you can repeat them up to four times, see if you feel anything new each time.

I couldn't believe it when the teacher said the next exercise was called the Downward Dog! When were we going to become warriors? I did ask, but the teacher replied that we need to feel and learn about our bodies' reactions to arrows of pain... with patience, we will get to be warriors soon.

She went on to explain that we can react similarly to dogs when threatened or in **danger**. Dogs can **whimper** and **curl up** and **shake**, or become **aggressive** – *growling*, BARKING and *snapping* at anyone!

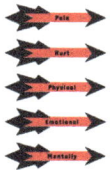

When we are having a difficult time, experiencing pain emotionally, physically or mentally, we can become bad-tempered. It can make us **niggly** and **snappy**, and **angry** – especially towards people who have not **hurt** us.

I knew that was true – I know I'm **horrible** to Mum when I'm **unhappy**. Even though sometimes all I want is a **hug**. ☹

PHYSICAL EXERCISE 3: The Downward Dog

Starting when you're ready in the **Cow** position, you may want to take an inhale. Try tucking your toes under and lifting your hips as high as is comfortable. You can bend you knees as little or as much as you would like.

You may feel some feelings in the back of your legs, in the muscles, and in your shoulders and arms. If this is uncomfortable, slightly adjust the movement or maybe return to the **Cow** position, then to **Child's Pose**, to relax.

If you are still in **Downward Dog**, are a happy dog today? If you like, you can wag your tail! And even woof!!If you are an unhappy dog, you can *grrrrowl* and BARK – see if it helps letting some of that unhappiness out!

You can choose how long you would like to stay in the Downward Dog pose. Remember to breathe and come down into Child's Pose when you are ready. Rest here for a few breaths.

The teacher explained that some battles we go into knowingly, but sometimes others pull us into a battle situation we don't want to be in, where we have no option but to fight our way out.

We got some more notes, which I think are interesting:

Going into Battle

Some battles you know how to deal with... but some are complicated, awkward, or may even seem too HUGE to deal with. At times like this we might try to ignore the problem, hoping it will go away, and lock everything inside. However, locking away our pain means the hurt can grow inside and can come out in other ways.

Like that angry dog, when you are feeling bad and you snap at or hurt another person, it is unlikely to make you feel any better, it will just make both of you feel bad.

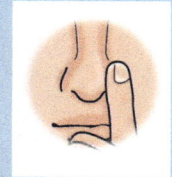

When you do feel those unhelpful feelings, you can try using the breathing and physical exercises we are doing until you can get your battle plan together.

Try to remember that everyone experiences arrows of pain and hurt.

You are not alone and you can find the strength and courage to get through this.

This can be really hard to remember, but is really important: if somebody hurts you, the problem lies with **THEM**, **not you**!

PHYSICAL EXERCISE 4: Mountain Pose

The best way to do this is to begin from the position of **Downward Dog** so when you're ready, come into **Downward Dog** and either walk your hands towards your feet or walk your feet towards your hands, until you're in a forward bend.

See how your body feels here. You can straighten your knees or keep a bend in your knees; whatever feels more comfortable for your body. Can you stay like this for a number of minutes? Maybe try focusing on your breathing.

When you are ready, you can place your hands onto your knees and straighten your back, maybe looking downwards, or forward.

I find this feels good for my body and back and I'm able to straighten my legs more here. Maybe you can think about how this feels for you?

If and when you are ready, you can bring your belly back towards your spine as you inhale. This will help support your spine, protecting it. With a straight back, in your own time, you can exhale as you rise up. If you would like to, you can stretch up high overhead.

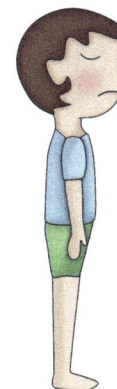

When you lower your arms, you can become solid - like a **Mountain**.

Try, if you like, to keep your feet firmly on the ground, feeling your leg muscles strengthen. See how it feels rolling your shoulders back, opening your chest. If this feels good, you can take a moment or two to breathe deeply, and feel the strength as a **Mountain**.

The teacher must have seen my face as I whispered to Sammy about wanting to do the **Warrior**. She said not to worry – we will become warriors next week as we need to do some homework first. We have to find out what it takes to become a warrior... and what the warrior movements represent and how they work.

Learning how to become a Warrior!

The warrior movements in yoga are called *Virabadrasana*:
Vira = 'Hero'
Bahadra = 'Friend'
Asana = 'Posture'

We may not always feel like it but we really do each have **inner warriors** that can be found. When we find them, we can become **warriors** for our own lives – our own hero friends.

The postures are similar in the fact that we have one or both feet grounded and strong. They all have one foot rooted or grounded in the past, the other leg bent and heading towards the future, and ourselves (the trunks of our bodies, our heads and our minds, strong and engaged in the present moment but gazing forward. Problems can arise in these poses if our bodies are leaning into the past or pushing into the future. This is also true for our thoughts so, whilst in the movements, trying to keep our mind in the present will take practice and focus!

All of the qualities below are within us; some may need a bit of work to find and develop, all will help you find and strengthen your inner warrior, ready to take on whatever life throws at you.

HONESTY: Free from lies, to be truthful and sincere in all you say and do.

BELIEF: Acceptance that something exists or is true, even when there is no proof.

KINDNESS: Being friendly, generous, and considerate of all living things.

HELPFULNESS: A willingness to support others.

RESILIENCE: Ability and determination to recover quickly from, or overcome, difficult conditions.

BRAVERY: Readiness to face unpleasant situations.

PRIDE: Recognition of, and satisfaction with, the results of achievements and qualities.

STRENGTH: Ability to withstand force and pressure.

EMPATHY: Ability to understand others' feelings and situations.

GIVING: Willingness to provide for others without expecting anything in return.

TRUE TO SELF: Being honest about your feelings, values and desires – with yourself and with others. Allowing truth to flow through you into the world.

Finally, this week, we were told that we could become actual warriors. We would be doing **Hero Friend** movements.

The teacher said something that I really liked: "Warriors stand **grounded**, **tall** and **fearless**. They stand with **one foot in the past** and **one pushing forwards into the future**. The body stands **straight** and **strong**, **centred in the present**."

This is what handout said, too, and I really like this idea – it takes you away from the bad things which have happened and stops you worrying about what might happen.

PHYSICAL EXERCISE 5: Warrior 1

I invite you to become a **Warrior**, starting from the **Mountain Pose** we ended with last week.

If you can, take one leg backwards, placing your foot at a 45-degree angle, being mindful of your body by directing your hips forwards.
How does it feel to keep both feet firmly grounded on the floor? Do you feel strong?

If you are ready, you can inhale and raise your arms above your head.
Try to relax if you feel any tension in your shoulders as sometimes we can tense up without realising. Exhaling may help release this.

When you feel your next inhale, maybe try bending your front knee forward, until it is aligned over your ankle. This is a strong movement. See how your body feels here for as long as up to six breaths. If you can only hold for a small time at first, don't worry – your body will get stronger with practice.

When you try holding this posture, you can add what is called a Positive Affirmation. Try saying - in your mind at first, if you prefer - loud and clearly:
"I am Tall and STRONG."

(It may feel a bit strange saying this to yourself so saying the words in your head is fine, but when you feel more confident it's great to say the words out loud. However you choose to say them, try to listen to those words and believe in them.)

When you are ready to come out of the pose, when you feel yourself inhale, straighten the bent knee then bring the back leg forwards, returning to Mountain Pose.

It is important in yoga to maintain a sense of balance, so when you are ready you can try repeating this exercise to the other side, with the opposite leg in front. Sometimes one side can seem stronger or easier than the other. Take note of this but it is nothing to worry about.

It was a bit strange, doing a **Positive Affirmation**, but Sammy was doing it so I thought I'd give it a go as well. When we did it, so did some of the others.

The teacher said that being a warrior means much more than possessing physical strength. It also means having an open heart, for honesty, truth, forgiveness and compassion.

PHYSICAL EXERCISE 6: Peace Warrior

Starting again from **Mountain Pose**, you can try taking one leg backwards as before and placing the foot again at a 45-degree angle with your hips facing forward, your feet placed firmly on the floor. See if you can feel the strength of your legs.

When you next feel an inhale, you can place one hands on your back leg, resting it on the back of the thigh.

When you are ready, as you start an exhale, you can try raising your other arm above your head, with the palm of your hand facing downward. Perhaps at same time you can bend your front knee forwards until it is in line with your ankle.

If you are comfortable to do so, it's safe to hold the pose for up to four breaths.

You can also try a Positive Affirmation here. Maybe:
"I open my heart for peace."

(As before, you can always say these words to yourself, in your own head, but when you are happy to say them out loud, you will be amazed by the effect).

Whenever you are ready to come out of the pose, you can try inhaling, straightening your bent knee and bringing the foot back to the centre, lowering your raised arm and bringing your other arm and back leg together, to finish once more on Mountain Pose.

As before, it's good to aim for balance so see if you can repeat the exercise to the opposite side.

We got to move on into another **Warrior Pose**, which was all to do with summoning our deepest strength, bravery, focus, and courage. **Ready to go into battle!!**

The teacher said that there is nothing wrong with feeling **afraid**, and that all warriors feel **fear** – and that sometimes **fear** is actually necessary in order to overcome problems. This really got me thinking.

PHYSICAL EXERCISE 7: Warrior 2

If you would like to practise how to go into battle, start again from **Mountain Pose**. When you are ready, as you have before, take one leg backward, placing your foot at a 45-degree angle, with strong legs, and hips facing firmly forwards.

When you feel the strength, and on your next inhale, try to raise both your arms parallel to your body.

Maybe in time, with your next exhale, start bending your front knee forward until it is above your ankle. Try not to bend it any further, to keep your body safe and well.

By feeling fear, we can use that energy to help summon courage and strength. We can help ourselves overcome the power any enemy or problem has over us. We can focus ahead, past them and to where they no longer can hurt us with their arrows. You can try this pose in front of a mirror (but remember, you are not focusing on yourself; you are not the problem. You look ahead, into the future, and see that your enemy or problem no longer has hold!). This I found helps me see past my problems and see a brighter time ahead.

Stay in this position for as long as you wish, up to six breaths.

Here you can try another Positive Affirmation:
"I am focused to overcome my fears!"

When you are ready to come out of the pose, inhale, and carefully return your legs and arms to their original **Mountain Pose** position.

Don't forget to maintain balance - try repeating this exercise to the opposite side.

When you have had a chance to try out these exercises, think about the following:

Which one of the three warriors have you felt the most benefit from?

Which one brings out the warrior in you?

The next exercise was **Warrior 3**, and that is all about responding to an attack by trying to be understanding and compassionate – towards ourselves as much as towards others.

The teacher said that this is NOT easy, and requires a lot of balance and focus. It's all about choosing how to react if we are **hurt** by an arrow of pain: we can either **lash out** in **anger**, or choose **balance**, **focus**, **understanding** and **compassion** inside first.

This exercise is to help us achieve this, to release any negative feeling around the pain or **hurt** for ourselves and others.

PHYSICAL EXERCISE: Warrior 3

If you would like to try this, you can start once more from the **Mountain Pose**.
First, try grounding one of your legs, which will be your standing leg. Keeping it strong, with a slightly bent knee. See how that feels.
Try to engage your belly back towards your spine; this can help you feel supported and strong.
Maybe on your next exhale, you can slowly tilt your top half forward from your hips, lifting your other leg straight back. See how that is for your body; if you wobble, just lower your leg until you find your balance. Remember, you are in control of your body and how far you go.

Once you find your balance, try putting your arms out either to the side to help, or out to the front, a bit like Superman or Supergirl flying! Your choice. It is absolutely fine to hold onto a wall, chair, or even another person to help you balance!

By checking our alignment, our engaged belly, our straight hips and our standing leg, it helps us to keep our safe and strong. Come out of this movement slowly whenever you feel you are losing balance.
How long can you hold your balance for? One breath? Two? Four? Even six??
It will become easier the more you practise.

A Positive Affirmation to try if you wish:
"I choose to respond to arrows with compassion and understanding for myself and others."

Maybe see how your balance on the opposite side; sometimes one side is stronger than the other.

19

There was one more exercise this week, which is called the **Humble Warrior**.

This is to do with times when we don't win a battle. Just because something hasn't worked out, it does not mean that we should give up – quite the opposite, in fact.

There can be many reasons that something hasn't gone right. The teacher suggested that maybe we needed more people to help, or that we could have done with a battle plan. We are going to look at these things next week.

The teacher also said that we needed to be able to take a step back, or retreat, to give us time and energy to reflect, recharge, gather reinforcements (like an army) and formulate a battle plan!

PHYSICAL EXERCISE 9: The Humble Warrior

As with the other **Warrior** poses, you can start with the **Mountain Pose** and take one leg backwards, placing the foot at a 45-degree angle.

With your hands behind your back, see if you can interlink your fingers.

When you exhale, you can try to bend your front knee forwards to above your ankle to help keep your body safe.

If you are comfortable, you can try bowing forward gently and lifting your arms up behind you.

You can stay in this position for as long as you wish, up to six breaths.

A Positive Affirmation which you can try is:

"I am confident to retreat, to restock, and to carry on!"

When you are ready, as you inhale, see if you can come back into the Mountain Pose.

Repeat the exercise on the other side to keep your body balanced.

I couldn't wait for yoga class this week. It's such a good change from our other lessons – even from sports, which I really love. I've been practising the exercises from the last three weeks, and I really think they are helping me.

We started off with a handout, and this one was really interesting - all to do with shields and armour. Sometimes I think I could do with both of these!

Every Warrior has Protection

Shields are a warrior's first defence. They provide protection from arrows. As we know, arrows can come in all shapes and sizes and can cause us pain mentally, physically and emotionally. A shield will help to protect us.

During times of battle, our inner warriors can carry the **Shield of True Reflection**. This is to provide protection and also show us the truth - that the arrows others fire are not because of anything we have done, said, or even thought.

The arrows come from others and the **Shield of True Reflection** teaches us that they are a reflection of the person firing them. They indicate that other person's weakness, and maybe pain of their own.

It takes great strength, empathy and kindness not to hurt others in return for the hurt we experience ourselves.

The **Shield of True Reflection** enables us to feel protected from pain inflicted by others, and gives us knowledge which will help to begin healing.

Armour is the warrior's second defence against the arrows of pain and hurt. It is a hard shell, protecting our soft bodies, feelings and emotions. However, if worn too long, heavy armour can weigh us down and keep us from positive experiences, as well as hiding away what is great and good about us.

Remember to only ever use your armour when in battle. When you remove it, you will feel like a weight has been lifted and you will be able to heal properly, and enjoy happy times.

Then we talked about having an army around us. The teacher said it is easy to feel alone with our problems and that others might not understand but that there will always be people who will want to help us if we ask.

Who we can call upon to join our Army!

It is important to remember that even though you are finding and developing your inner warrior, you do not have to fight your battles alone.

There are a lot of people around who can help. Below are just a few.

Take a minute or two to think of some people who could be in your army. I bet you'll find there are far more than you might first think. If you find it hard to say out loud what is bothering you, try to think of another way to communicate. Some people find writing things down – or even emailing or texting - easier. It does not matter how you do it – just that you do.

Mum/Dad/Step-Parent/Foster-Parent/Carer: It can be really difficult – even scary! – asking parents for help. You just know that they are going to ask you loads of questions and they might become upset or worried themselves. You may be concerned that they won't believe you. However, remember that parents and carers want you to be safe, healthy and happy. They might seem busy, but believe me, they would want to know if you are upset. Once your parent or carer knows what is going on, they will be a key member of your army!

Teacher/Sports Coach/Youth Worker: If you have another adult in your life who you like and trust, they can also be in a brilliant position to help you. People with jobs like these are trained to help and support young people. They are fully qualified for a position in your army.

Siblings/grandparents/cousins/other family members: You might argue with your brother or sister; you may not see your cousin, aunt or uncle very often, but your family love you and care about you. Grandparents can seem a world away from what you are experiencing but remember, they have been young and they may even have experienced something similar to what is happening to you. They will want to help you, and want to line up by your side with your other soldiers!

Childline: If you really feel like you can't find people who you know that you can turn to, there is still somewhere to go. Childline is a free, completely confidential, service which is for ALL children in the UK under 19 years of age. There are friendly, understanding, trained counsellors who can talk to you about ANY issue - no matter how big or small. You can call them on 0800 1111 for FREE at any time, or contact them online at www.childline.org.uk.

999/Police: The job of the Police Force is to protect people from harm. If you feel you are in danger, or are in fear of being hurt, you can call 999. They are trained officers that will listen to you and are able to help you.

I was starting to **worry** that we weren't going to do any yoga this week, when the teacher said we were going to do some exercises with partners. I chose Alex, who is calm and sensible, and won't try to make me laugh like I know Robin will.

The teacher explained how having an army is always important when fighting battles. Sometimes just a small army will do, and sometimes we need a lot of people working together to win a battle. Listening, communication and trust are key.

There were two exercises to try. I was right to choose Alex. Sammy had Robin, and they ended up falling over in the second exercise. They couldn't stop laughing. I kind of felt like I'd like to be messing about with them but I really want to know if yoga can help me sort out my problems.

PHYSICAL EXERCISE 10: Warrior 2s Together

If you wish to try this pose start by standing side-by-side, place your inner feet touching. Together, move your outside legs out so that your feet are apart. You will notice your inner feet anchor against each other for support and both inner and outer feet are firmly grounded.
Try holding onto each other's wrists, of your inner hands, only for support. Wrists are stronger than slippery hands.
By talking to each other, you can decide together when to exhale, and bend your outer knees whilst straightening your arms.
Turn to look away from each other.

What can you feel? Do you feel supported by your friend? Do you feel stronger separate or together? Maybe use another Positive Affirmation together:

"We friends feel strong and supported together."

Deciding together when you are both happy to return to your original pose and maybe swap positions and try the same exercise using your opposite sides.

PHYSICAL EXERCISE 11: Warrior 3s Together

Start by standing facing each other. Place your hands on your partner's shoulders.

Slowly, together, walk backwards, until your arms are outstretched.

By talking to each other, you can choose a 'standing leg' which, as you look at each other, will be opposite to your partner's. You can then try and slowly lift the other leg from the floor, backwards, so that your bodies tilt forwards... try not to bang heads!

You can support each other to maintain balance.

If you feel wobbly, come down slowly, and try on the other leg...

When you have had a chance to try these exercises, think about the following:

Which one works better for you, and why?

How did you feel, working with a partner? Were you stronger together?

The last exercise was great – though I didn't like the idea of it at first. After a few words from the teacher, even Robin stopped messing about and we all said we **enjoyed** it.

PHYSICAL EXERCISE 12: The Trust Circle

Trust is an integral part in building an army and letting someone in to help you in your battle.
Let's practise letting go, trusting and supporting each other, creating a Trust Circle. You will need some members of your army for this exercise and should be supervised by an adult.

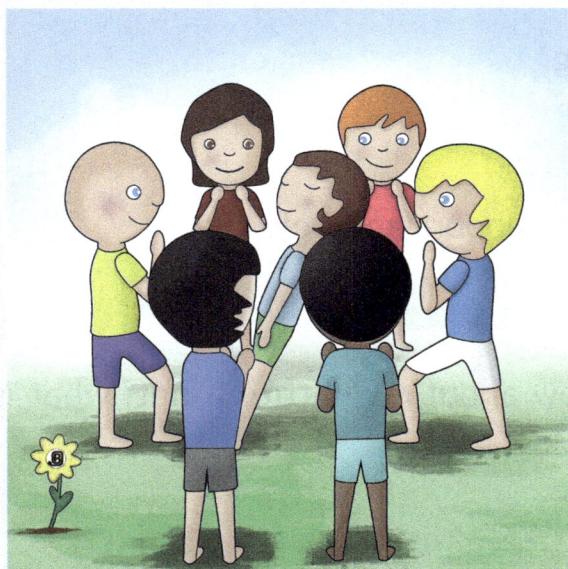

One person stands in the middle whilst everyone else stands in a circle around them, each touching shoulders with the people next to them.
Everyone in the circle steps one leg back slightly, so that they have grounding to push against.
Each person in the circle should then put their hands up, palms facing inside the circle.
The person in the middle crosses their arms over their body and closes their eyes. They can then let themselves go and fall in any direction.

This is not an easy thing to do!

By placing your trust in the members of your circle, you will see that there are people who will catch you, support you, and get you upright again.

A great **Positive Affirmation** for this exercise is:
"I believe in and trust in my support."

You can try this with each member of the circle taking a turn in the middle.

If you don't feel comfortable, that is fine. Enjoy being there, supporting your friends.

Afterwards, we talked about having a battle plan. I think this will really help me.
We didn't have to write a plan down if we didn't want to – and I didn't. But we got a handout about it so I know what my plan is.

BATTLE PLANS

To prepare for battle we need to have a plan.

Some things we may need to consider:
Who is involved in my problems?

What are they doing?

Who in my army can support and help me?

Do they already know about my battle? If not, what is the best way to tell them?

When is the best time to ask somebody to join my army?

Once you know who you would like to be in your army, you need to ask them to help.

Maybe you can only think of one trusted adult, but they in turn may know other people who you have never even thought of.
If you are worried about this, talk to them about it. I am sure they will talk this through with you fully first before enlisting further help.
Remember the **breathing exercises** from earlier in the book. These will help you become calm and soothe any worries before you talk to somebody.

I know what the problem is – which is that person I mentioned earlier.

I know how they make me feel: **scared**, **sick** and **anxious**.

I need to think about my army: I want to tell Mum, but she's so busy, and I'm worried about **upsetting** her.

I came up with a solution. I called Childline, to ask how I could speak to my mum. I felt really nervous ringing them but they were great. I also used some of the breathing exercises before I phoned so that I could try and stay **calm**. I think it helped. It was much, much easier than I thought it would be.

I told them what we had been doing at school, with yoga, and I told them about the breathing diary. They said I could use this to show Mum, and I did. And I showed Mum some of the warrior exercises! Now Mum is going to help me get my army together.

I have practised and can now tune into my body more easily. I can recognise my feelings now and where in my body I feel them, and how to breathe to help release them!

Visualising the **armour** and the **Shield of True Reflection**, I can help protect myself by knowing that what has happened is not a reflection of me but the person who has **hurt** me.

I don't feel so **angry** anymore, which means I am not so **snappy** at Mum, which is good.

Most importantly, I listen to and trust the feelings in my gut so I know when something is wrong.

I also know what I can do about it!! I start to **breathe**, **feel**, **write a battle plan**, and **get my army together**.

All is good now... and now I am using this book to help me heal along with help from a counsellor, who is now a member of my army too.

This week we have been talking about **healing through yoga**, which is perfect for me, now that I am dealing with the problems I've been having.

This is just as important as fighting those battles. The teacher says that everyone deserves to be happy and that even the best ever **Warriors** still get hit by arrows of **hurt** and pain from time to time.

We did the **Hero** and **Camel** poses. I liked the sound of the **Hero** one, but wasn't so sure about the **Camel**! But apparently they are both designed to help us open our hearts, which is the first step to **healing**.

The teacher said to focus on your own heart, opening it and letting out any **hurt**, **anger**, or **sadness** that we might feel. Also that we should treat ourselves with **kindness** and **compassion**, as we would treat others the same.

RELAXATION & HEALING EXERCISE 1: The Hero Pose

You have found your **inner warrior** and now you need to feel like the **hero** you are.

Sit down if you can, resting back onto your feet. You can place your hands on the floor and have your fingers pointing towards you or away from you; this is entirely your choice.

Then when you're ready, bend backwards really slowly.
Notice how you are opening your chest, ready to receive love, healing and compassion.

Breathe deeply and feel how good it is to open up this way.

Positive Affirmation:

"I am helping my body, mind and spirit heal from the battle."

When you feel you want to come out of this pose, as you inhale slowly, roll back up and sit back on your feet. You can repeat the exercise if you would like.

RELAXATION & HEALING EXERCISE 2: The Camel Pose

To progress from **Hero**, rise off your lower legs, so you are on your knees, then tuck your toes under so that now your ankles are up above your toes.

As you inhale, place your hands on your lower, back ready for an exhale, where you can slowly bend backwards so that your heart is facing the sky!

You can see if you can lower your hands so that they reach down and hold onto the heels of your feet. If that is too much of a bend, slowly rise back up to put your hands on your lower back.
Breathe slowly and focus on receiving healing, love and compassion.

To come out of this pose you can inhale slowly, rolling back up and sitting back on your feet.

Positive Affirmation:

"I am helping my body, mind and spirit heal from the battle."
Again, if you feel you would like to repeat the exercise, please do.

Once the warrior's heart is healed, they need to rest, relax and restore their energy, nurturing themselves. A great way to do this, after the Hero or the Camel Pose, is to go into Child's Pose.

Positive Affirmation:

"I feel calm and peaceful."

Then we had some stretching exercises to try. The teacher said that stretching is very important for warriors, as muscles need to lengthen and relax whilst reaching and stretching.

RELAXATION & HEALING EXERCISE 3: Seated Side-Stretch

Come to sitting with one leg stretched out to the side.

Try bending your other leg and see if you can you bring the sole of your foot to the top of your stretched leg, or wherever it is comfortable for your body.

With your hips sideways, as you inhale, see if you can raise the same arm as your bent leg then on your next exhale, try slowly bending over your stretched leg.

Maybe place the other hand down on to your stretched leg or onto your toes if it is comfortable.

Think about your heart, and your breathing, and stay in this position as long or as little as you like for up to six breaths. Where can you feel that stretch?

Possibly try to repeat to the other side and feel your stretch on that side of your body.

The teacher talked more about our central nervous systems, and how we can relax them.

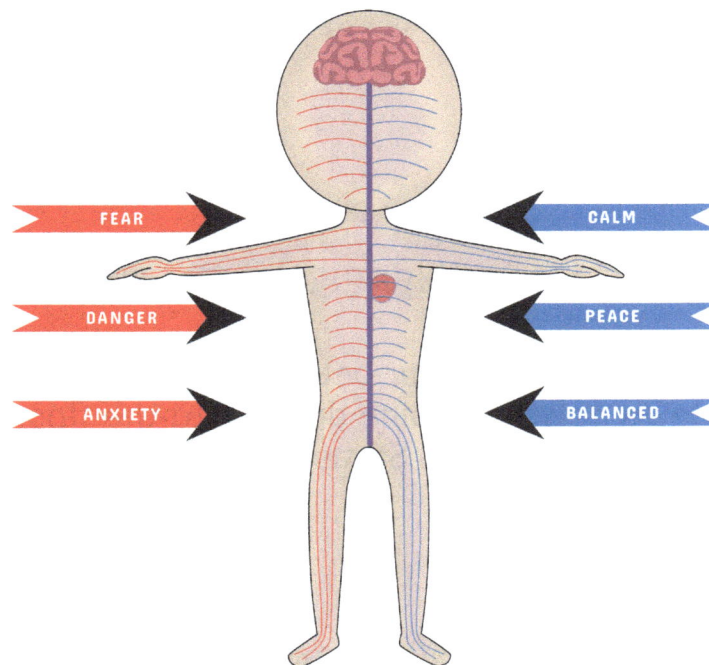

FEAR

DANGER

ANXIETY

CALM

PEACE

BALANCED

The next exercise is meant to help relax this system and is similar to the **standing forward bend**.

RELAXATION & HEALING EXERCISE 4: Seated Forward Bend

If it's comfortable to do so, sit with both legs out in front of you. Your knees can be bent a lot, a little, or straight, see how you are feeling right now.

As you inhale, see if you can raise your arms over your head. Then, as you exhale, slowly bend forwards, from your waist over your legs.

You can rest your hands on your legs, toes, wherever they land; make sure you are comfortable.

With your head down, breathe and relax, and you are welcome to stay in this position for up to six breaths. How does that feel?

To come out of pose, pull your belly towards your back again to help support your back, raise up to the seated position, and lower your arms back to your sides.

Finally, it was time to relax.

RELAXATION & HEALING EXERCISE 5: Time for Relaxation...

As you inhale, you can engage your belly towards your back.
As you exhale, slowly roll your spine down onto the floor, until you are lying on your back on the mat, in Savasana.

Legs are outstretched. Notice how your feet may roll outward, or you can put the soles of your feet together, knees apart in reclining butterfly; whichever is comfortable for you.

See how your shoulders feel; maybe relax them down your back and experiment with your arms either lying along the side of your body or on your body. Do whatever feels best for you. If you aren't comfortable, you won't relax properly.

Maybe take a few deep tummy breaths here and take this time to tune in to your body, your mind and your breathing.

Savasana is not a sleeping pose but a restorative pose which helps our mind and body rest and restore.

Use this space to make some notes about what you've found as you have tried the exercises in this book.

How does your body feel? Can you feel any tension, aches, or pains? How about your emotions, or thoughts?

Have you discovered anything which you think might be helpful in dealing with any problems and difficulties in life?

As it was our last class, the teacher had a special surprise for each of us – a CD which we can take home.
It says on the cover:

All warriors need a special time for themselves!

It can help absorb the benefits from breathing, learning and yoga exercises.

This is a special time to help the mind, body and feelings to reflect, rest and restore.

She put it on as we relaxed and it was amazing! She got us to find our own safe space inside our minds where all our worries can melt away... really! I felt **brilliant** afterwards: **calm**, **loved** and **happy**.

It was now the end of becoming warriors and I was worried that would be the end of yoga in school ☹. The teacher explained she would be back and next time we will learn to open our 'wings of change' - whatever that meant?? However, I was happy that it was not the end at all!

She taught us a saying they use in yoga, saying we could use it to acknowledge each other:

THE LIGHT, PEACE AND LOVE IN ME...
SEES THE LIGHT, PEACE AND LOVE IN YOU...

You can download the Safe Space Relaxation Audio for FREE by visiting:

www.believe-in.co.uk/Believe-in-your-inner-warrior/safe-space

Lightning Source UK Ltd.
Milton Keynes UK
UKOW07f2130140517
301142UK00001B/1/P